Everyone Needs Someone

Everyone Needs Someone

POEMS OF LOVE AND FRIENDSHIP

Helen Steiner Rice

Fleming H. Revell Company   Old Tappan, New Jersey

Published by Pyramid Publications for the Fleming H. Revell Company
Revell edition published September 1973
    Fifth printing February 1977
ISBN 0-8007-0669-2

Graphic design by Paul Bacon

Fleming H. Revell Company
Old Tappan, New Jersey 07675, U.S.A.

Contents

Everyone Needs Someone

THE MAGIC OF LOVE 8
WHAT IS MARRIAGE? 10
LOVE ONE ANOTHER FOR LOVE IS OF GOD 12
EVERYONE NEEDS SOMEONE 14
THERE'S SUNSHINE IN A SMILE 15
WHERE THERE IS LOVE 16
WHEN TWO PEOPLE MARRY 18
THE POWER OF LOVE 20
GIVE LAVISHLY! LIVE ABUNDANTLY! 22
WHAT IS LOVE? 24
STRANGERS ARE FRIENDS WE HAVEN'T MET 26
THE PRICELESS GIFT 28

Gifts from the Heart

THE GIFT OF FRIENDSHIP 32
HEART GIFTS 34
HELP YOURSELF TO HAPPINESS 36
A SURE WAY TO A HAPPY DAY 37
A FAVORITE RECIPE 38
MAKE YOUR DAY BRIGHT BY THINKING RIGHT 40
THE ANSWER 42

A THANKFUL HEART 44
"FLOWERS LEAVE THEIR FRAGRANCE ON THE HAND THAT BESTOWS THEM" 46

Daily Thoughts for Daily Needs

NEW BEGINNINGS 50
GIVE US DAILY AWARENESS 52
HOW GREAT THE YIELD FROM A FERTILE FIELD 54
ON THE WINGS OF PRAYER 56
THANK GOD FOR LITTLE THINGS 58
MY GOD IS NO STRANGER 60
BEYOND OUR ASKING 62
FULFILLMENT 64
HE LOVES YOU! 66
NEVER BORROW SORROW FROM TOMORROW 68
THINGS TO BE THANKFUL FOR 70
GOD KNOWS BEST 72
EVERYBODY EVERYWHERE NEEDS SOMEBODY SOMETIME 74
"DEAR FRIENDS"—A WORD FROM THE AUTHOR 77

Everyone Needs Someone

The Magic of Love

Love is like *magic*
And it always will be,
For love still remains
Life's sweet mystery!

Love works in ways
That are wondrous and strange
And there's *nothing in life*
That *love cannot change!*

Love can transform
The most commonplace
Into beauty and splendor
And sweetness and grace!

Love is unselfish,
Understanding and kind,
For it sees with its *heart*
And not with its mind!

Love is the answer
That everyone seeks—
Love is the language
That every heart speaks—

Love can't be bought,
It is priceless and free,
Love like pure *magic*
Is a *sweet mystery!*

What Is Marriage?

Marriage is the union
    of two people in love,
And love is sheer magic
    for it's woven of
Gossamer dreams,
    enchantingly real,
That people in love
    are privileged to feel—
But the "exquisite ecstasy"
    that captures the heart
Of two people in love
    is just a small part
Of the beauty and wonder
    and *miracle* of
The growth and fulfillment
    and evolvement of love—
For only long years
    of living together

And sharing and caring
    in all kinds of weather
Both pleasure and pain,
    the glad and the sad,
Teardrops and laughter,
    the good and the bad,
Can add new dimensions
    and lift love above
The rapturous ecstasies
    of "falling in love"—
For ecstasy passes
    but it is replaced
By something much greater
    that cannot be defaced,
For what was "in part"
    has now "become whole"—
For on the "wings of the flesh,"
    love entered the "soul"!

Love One Another for Love Is

Every couple should remember
    that what the world calls love
Is not something man invented,
    but it comes from God above ...
And love can be neglected
    and oftentimes abused,
Perverted and distorted,
    misguided and misused,
Or it can be developed
    by living every day
Near to God, *Our Father,*
    and following in *His Way* ...
For God alone can teach you
    the meaning of true love,

And He can help establish
    the life you're dreaming of
In which you live together
    in happiness and peace,
Enjoying married blessings
    that day by day increase ...
For love that is immortal
    has its source in God above,
And the love you give each other
    is founded on His love ...
And though upon *your wedding day*
    it seems *yours* and *yours alone,*
If you but ask, God takes *your love*
    and blends it with *His Own.*

of God

Everyone Needs Someone

People need people
    and friends need friends,
And we all need love
    for a full life depends
Not on vast riches
    or great acclaim,
Not on success
    or on worldly fame,
But just in knowing
    that someone cares
And holds us close
    in their thoughts and prayers—
For only the knowledge
    that we're understood
Makes everyday living
    feel *wonderfully good,*

And we rob ourselves
    of life's greatest need
When we "lock up our hearts"
    and fail to heed
The outstretched hand
    reaching to find
A kindred spirit
    whose heart and mind
Are lonely and longing
    to somehow share
Our joys and sorrows
    and to make us aware
That life's completeness
    and richness depends
On the things we share
    with our loved ones and friends.

Life is a mixture
    of sunshine and rain,
Laughter and pleasure,
    teardrops and pain,
All days can't be bright,
    but it's certainly true,
There was never a cloud
    the sun didn't shine through—
So just keep on smiling
    whatever betide you,
Secure in the knowledge
    God is always beside you,

And you'll find when you smile
    your day will be brighter
And all of your burdens
    will seem so much lighter—
For each time you smile
    you will find it is true
Somebody, somewhere
    will *smile back at you,*
And nothing on earth
    can make life more worthwhile
Than the sunshine and warmth
    of a *beautiful smile.*

There's Sunshine in a Smile

Where There Is Love

Where there is love the heart is light,
Where there is love the day is bright,
Where there is love there is a song
To help when things are going wrong...
Where there is love there is a smile
To make all things seem more worthwhile,
Where there is love there's quiet peace,
A tranquil place where turmoils cease—
Love changes darkness into light
And makes the heart take "wingless flight"...
Oh, blest are they who walk in love,
They also walk with God above—
And when you walk with God each day
And kneel together when you pray,
Your marriage will be truly blest
And God will be your daily *"guest"*—
And love that once seemed yours alone,
God gently blends into *His Own*.

When Two People Marry

Your hearts are filled with happiness
    so great and overflowing,
You cannot comprehend it
    for it's far beyond all knowing
How any heart could hold such joy
    or feel the fullness of
The wonder and the glory
    and the ecstasy of love—
You wish that you could capture it
    and never let it go
So you might walk forever
    in its radiant magic glow . . .
But love in all its ecstasy
    is such a fragile thing,
Like gossamer in cloudless skies
    or a hummingbird's small wing,
But love that lasts *forever*
    must be made of something strong,

The kind of strength that's gathered
    when the heart can hear no song—
When the "sunshine" of your wedding day
    runs into "stormy weather"
And hand in hand you brave the gale
    and climb steep hills together,
And clinging to each other
    while the thunder rolls above
You seek divine protection
    in *Faith* and *Hope* and *Love* . . .
For *"days of wine and roses"*
    never make love's dream come true,
It takes sacrifice and teardrops,
    and problems shared by two,
To give true love its *beauty*,
    its *grandeur* and its *fineness*
And to mold an "earthly ecstasy"
    into *Heavenly divineness*.

The Power of Love

There is no thinking person
    who can stand untouched today
And view the world around us
    drifting downward to decay
Without feeling deep within them
    a silent unnamed dread,
Wondering how to stem the chaos
    that lies frightfully ahead . . .
But the problems we are facing
    cannot humanly be solved
For our diplomatic strategy
    only gets us more involved
And our skillful ingenuity,
    our technology and science

Can never change a sinful heart
    filled with hatred and defiance . . .
So our problems keep on growing
    every hour of every day
As man vainly tries to solve them
    in his own *self-willful way* . . .
But man is powerless alone
    to *clean up the world outside*
Until his own polluted soul
    is *clean* and *free inside* . . .
For the amazing power of love
    is beyond all comprehension
And it alone can heal this world
    of its hatred and dissension.

Give Lavishly! Live Abundantly!

The more you give, the more you get—
The more you laugh, the less you fret—
The more you do *unselfishly*,
The more you live *abundantly* . . .

The more of everything you share,
The more you'll always have to spare—
The more you love, the more you'll find
That life is good and friends are kind . . .

For only *what we give away,*
Enriches us from day to day.

What Is Love?

What is love?
> No words can define it.
It's something so great
> Only God could design it...
Wonder of Wonders,
> Beyond man's conception,
And only in God
> Can love find true perfection.
For love means much more
> Than small words can express,
For what man calls love
> Is so very much less

Than the beauty and depth
> And the true richness of
God's gift to mankind—
> His compassionate love...
For love has become
> A word that's misused,
Perverted, distorted
> And often abused.
To speak of "light romance"
> Or some affinity for
A passing attraction
> That is seldom much more

Than a mere interlude
      Of inflamed fascination,
A romantic fling
      Of no lasting duration...
But love is enduring
      And patient and kind.
It judges all things
      With the heart, not the mind.
And love can transform
      The most commonplace
Into beauty and splendor
      And sweetness and grace...

For love is unselfish,
      Giving more than it takes,
And no matter what happens
      Love never forsakes.
It's faithful and trusting
      And always believing,
Guileless and honest
      And never deceiving...
Yes, love is beyond
      What man can define,
For love is Immortal
      And God's Gift is Divine!

Strangers Are Friends We Haven't Met

God knows *no strangers,* He loves us all,
    the poor, the rich, the great, the small . . .
He is a friend who is always there
    to share our troubles and lessen our care . . .
No one is a stranger in God's sight,
    for *God is love* and in *His light*
May we, too, try in our small way
    to make *new friends* from day to day . . .
So pass no stranger with an unseeing eye,
    for God may be sending a *new friend by.*

The Priceless Gift

The priceless gift of life is love,
For with the help of God above
Love can change the human race
And make this world a better place—
For love dissolves all hate and fear
And makes our vision bright and clear
So we can see and rise above
Our pettiness on "wings of love."

Gifts from the Heart

The Gift of Friendship

Friendship is a *priceless gift*
    that cannot be bought or sold,
But its value is far greater
    than a mountain made of gold—
For gold is cold and lifeless,
    it can neither see nor hear,
And in the time of trouble
    it is powerless to cheer—
It has no ears to listen,
    no heart to understand,
It cannot bring you comfort
    or reach out a helping hand—
So when you ask God for a *gift,*
    be thankful if *He* sends
Not diamonds, pearls or riches,
    but the love of real true friends.

Heart Gifts

It's not the things that can be bought
        that are life's richest treasure,
It's just the little "heart gifts"
        that money cannot measure . . .
A cheerful smile, a friendly word,
        a sympathetic nod
Are priceless little treasures
        from the storehouse of our God . . .
They are the things that can't be bought
        with silver or with gold,
For thoughtfulness and kindness
        and love are never sold . . .
They are the priceless things in life
        for which no one can pay,
And the giver finds rich recompense
        in *giving them away*.

Help Yourself to Happiness

Everybody, everywhere
    seeks happiness, it's true,
But finding it and keeping it
    seems difficult to do,
Difficult because we think
    that happiness is found
Only in the places where
    wealth and fame abound—
And so we go on searching
    in "palaces of pleasure"
Seeking recognition
    and monetary treasure,
Unaware that happiness
    is just a "state of mind"
Within the reach of everyone
    who takes time to be kind—
For in making *others happy*
    we will be happy, too,
For the happiness you give away
    returns to "shine on you."

A Sure Way to a Happy Day

Happiness is something
    we create in our mind,
It's not something you search for
    and so seldom find—
It's just waking up
    and beginning the day
By counting our blessings
    and kneeling to pray—
It's giving up thoughts
    that breed discontent
And accepting what comes
    as a "gift heaven-sent"—

It's giving up wishing
    for things we have not
And making the best of
    whatever we've got—
It's knowing that life
    is determined for us,
And pursuing our tasks
    without fret, fume or fuss—
For it's by completing
    what God gives us to do
That we find real contentment
    and happiness, too.

A Favorite Recipe

Take a *cup* of *Kindness,*
mix it well with *Love,*
Add a lot of Patience
and *Faith* in *God above,*
Sprinkle very generously
with *Joy* and *Thanks* and *Cheer*—
And you'll have lots of *"Angel Food"*
to feast on all the year.

Make Your Day

Bright by Thinking Right

Don't start your day by supposin'
    that trouble is just ahead,
It's better to stop supposin'
    and start with a prayer instead,
And make it a prayer of *thanksgiving*
    for the wonderful things God has wrought
Like the beautiful sunrise and sunset,
    "God's gifts" that are free
    and not bought—
For what is the use of supposin'
    the dire things that could happen to you
And worry about some misfortune
    that seldom if ever comes true—

But instead of just idle supposin'
    step forward to meet each new day
Secure in the knowledge God's near you
    to lead you each step of the way—
For supposin' the worst things will happen
    only helps to make them come true
And you darken the bright, happy moments
    that the dear Lord has given to you—
So if you desire to be happy
    and get rid of the *"misery* of *dread"*
Just give up *"supposin' the worst things"*
    and look for *"the best things"* instead.

 The Answer

In the tiny petal
    of a tiny flower
        that grew from a tiny pod . . .
Is the *miracle*
    and the *mystery*
        of *all creation* and *God!*

A Thankful Heart

Take nothing for granted,
  for whenever you do
The "joy of enjoying"
  is lessened for you—
For we rob our own lives
  much more than we know
When we fail to respond
  or in any way show
Our thanks for the blessings
  that daily are ours . . .
The warmth of the sun,
  the fragrance of flowers,
The beauty of twilight,
  the freshness of dawn,
The coolness of dew
  on a green velvet lawn,

The kind little deeds
  so thoughtfully done,
The favors of friends
  and the love that someone
Unselfishly gives us
  in a myriad of ways,
Expecting no payment
  and no words of praise—
Oh, great is our loss
  when we no longer find
A thankful response
  to things of this kind,
For the *joy of enjoying*
  and the *Fullness of living*
Are found in the heart
  that is filled with *Thanksgiving*.

"Flowers Leave Their Fragrance on the Hand That Bestows Them"

There's an old Chinese proverb
    that, if practiced each day,
Would change the whole world
    in a wonderful way—
Its truth is so simple,
    it's so easy to do,
And it works every time
    and successfully, too . . .
For you can't do a kindness
    without a reward,
Not in silver nor gold
    but in joy from the Lord—
You can't light a candle
    to show others the way
Without feeling the warmth
    of that bright little ray . . .
And you can't pluck a rose,
    all fragrant with dew,
Without part of its fragrance
    remaining with you.

Daily Thoughts
for
Daily Needs

New Beginnings

How often we wish for another chance
To make a fresh beginning,
A chance to blot out our mistakes
And change failure into winning—
And it does not take a new year
To make a brand-new start,
It only takes the deep desire
To try with all our heart
To live a little better
And to always be forgiving
And to add a little "sunshine"
To the world in which we're living—
So never give up in despair
And think that you are through,
For there's always a tomorrow
And a chance to start anew.

Give Us Daily Awareness

On life's busy thoroughfares
We meet with angels unawares—
So, Father, make us kind and wise
So we may always recognize
The blessings that are ours to take,
The friendships that are ours to make
If we but open our heart's door wide
To let the sunshine of love inside.

The farmer ploughs through the fields of green
And the blade of the plough is sharp and keen,
But the seed must be sown to bring forth grain,
For nothing is born without suffering and pain—
And God never ploughs in the soul of man
Without intention and purpose and plan,
So whenever you feel the plough's sharp blade
Let not your heart be sorely afraid
For, like the farmer, God chooses a field
From which He expects an excellent yield—
So rejoice though your heart is broken in two,
God seeks to bring forth a rich harvest in you.

a Fertile Field

On the Wings of Prayer

Just close your eyes
    and open your heart
And feel your worries
    and cares depart,
Just yield yourself
    to the Father above
And let Him hold you
    secure in His love ...
For life on earth
    grows more involved
With endless problems
    that can't be solved—
But God only asks us
    to do our best,
Then He will "take over"
    and finish the rest ...
So when you are tired,
    discouraged and blue,
There's always one door
    that is open to you—

And that is the door
    to *"The House of Prayer"*
And you'll find God waiting
    to meet you there ...
And *"The House of Prayer"*
    is no farther away
Than the quiet spot
    where you kneel and pray—
For the heart is a temple
    when God is there
As we place ourselves
    in His loving care.
And He hears every prayer
    and answers each one
When we pray in His name
    "Thy will be done"—
And the burdens that seemed
    too heavy to bear
Are lifted away
    on *"the wings of prayer."*

Thank God for Little Things

Thank you, God, for little things
       that often come our way—
The things we take for granted
       but don't mention when we pray—
The unexpected courtesy,
       the thoughtful, kindly deed—
A hand reached out to help us
       in the time of sudden need—
Oh make us more aware, dear God,
       of little daily graces
That come to us with "sweet surprise"
       from never-dreamed-of places.

My God Is

I've never seen God,
     but I know how I feel...
It's people like *you*
     who make *Him* *"so real"*...
My God is no stranger,
     He's friendly and gay...

And *He* doesn't ask me
     to weep when I pray...
It seems that I pass *Him*
     so often each day...
In the faces of people
     I meet on my way...

No Stranger

He's the stars in the heaven,
  a smile on some face...
A leaf on a tree
  or a rose in a vase...
He's winter and autumn
  and summer and spring...

In short, *God Is Every*
  Real, Wonderful Thing...
I wish I might meet *Him*
  much more than I do...
I would if there were
  more people like you.

Beyond Our Asking

More than hearts can imagine
    or minds comprehend,
God's bountiful gifts
    are ours without end—
We ask for a cupful
    when the vast sea is ours,
We pick a small rosebud
    from a garden of flowers,
We reach for a sunbeam
    but the sun still abides,
We draw one short breath
    but there's air on all sides—

Whatever we ask for
    falls short of God's giving
For *His greatness* exceeds
    every facet of living,
And always God's ready
    and eager and willing
To pour out His mercy
    completely fulfilling
All of man's needs
    for peace, joy and rest
For God gives His children
    whatever is best—

Just give Him a chance
        to open *His treasures*
And He'll fill your life
        with unfathomable pleasures,
Pleasures that never
        grow worn-out and faded
And leave us depleted,
        disillusioned and jaded—
For God has a "storehouse"
        just filled to the brim
With all that man needs
        if we'll only ask Him.

Fulfillment

Apple blossoms bursting wide
    now beautify the tree
And make a Springtime picture
    that is beautiful to see . . .
Oh, fragrant lovely blossoms,
    you'll make a bright bouquet
If I but break your branches
    from the apple tree today . . .
But if I break your branches
    and make your beauty mine,
You'll bear no fruit in season
    when severed from the vine . . .

And when we cut ourselves away
    from guidance that's divine,
Our lives will be as fruitless
    as the branch without the vine . . .
For as the flowering branches
    depend upon the tree
To nourish and fulfill them
    till they reach futurity,
We too must be dependent
    on our Father up above,
For we are but the *branches*
    and He's *the tree of love.*

He Loves You!

It's amazing and incredible,
But it's as true as it can be,
God loves and understands us all
And that means *you* and *me*—
His grace is all sufficient
For both the *young* and *old,*
For the lonely and the timid,
For the brash and for the bold—
His love knows no exceptions,
So never feel excluded

No matter *who* or *what* you are
Your name has been included—
And no matter what your past has been,
Trust God to understand,
And no matter what your problem is
Just place it in His Hand—
For in all of our *unloveliness*
This *Great God loves us still,*
He loved us since the world began
And what's more, *He always will!*

Never
Borrow
Sorrow
from
Tomorrow

Deal only with the present,
Never step into tomorrow,
For God asks us just to trust Him
And to never borrow sorrow—
For the future is not ours to know
And it may never be,
So let us live and give our best
And give it lavishly—
For to meet tomorrow's troubles
Before they are even ours
Is to anticipate the Saviour
And to doubt His all-wise powers—
So let us be content to solve
Our problems one by one,
Asking nothing of tomorrow
Except *"Thy Will be done."*

Things to Be

Thankful For

The good, green earth beneath our feet,
The air we breathe, the food we eat,
Some work to do, a goal to win,
A hidden longing deep within
That spurs us on to bigger things
And helps us meet what each day brings,
All these things and many more
Are things we should be thankful for . . .
And most of all our thankful prayers
Should rise to God because He cares!

God Knows Best

Our Father knows what's best for us,
So why should we complain—
We always want the sunshine,
But He knows there must be rain—
We love the sound of laughter
And the merriment of cheer,
But our hearts would lose their tenderness
If we never shed a tear . . .
Our Father tests us often
With suffering and with sorrow,
He tests us, not to punish us,
But to help us meet *tomorrow* . . .

For growing trees are strengthened
When they withstand the storm,
And the sharp cut of the chisel
Gives the marble grace and form . . .
God never hurts us needlessly,
And He never wastes our pain,
For every loss He sends to us
Is followed by rich gain . . .
And when we count the blessings
That God has so freely sent,

We will find no cause for murmuring
And no time to lament . . .
For Our Father loves His children,
And to Him all things are plain,
So He never sends us *pleasure*
When the *soul's deep need is pain* . . .
So whenever we are troubled,
And when everything goes wrong,
It is just God working in us
To make *our spirit strong.*

Everybody Everywhere Needs Somebody Sometime

Everybody, everywhere,
    no matter what his station,
Has moments of deep loneliness
    and quiet desperation,
For this lost and lonely feeling
    is inherent in mankind—
It is just the *Spirit speaking*
    as God tries again to find
An opening in the "worldly wall"
    man builds against God's touch,

For he feels so self-sufficient
    that he does not need God much,
So he vainly goes on struggling
    to find some explanation
For these disturbing, lonely moods
    of inner isolation ...
But the answer keeps eluding him
    for in his selfish, finite mind
He does not even recognize
    that he cannot ever find

The reason for life's emptiness
    unless he learns to share
The problems and the burdens
    that surround him everywhere—
But when his eyes are opened
    and he looks with love at others
He begins to see not *strangers*
    but understanding brothers . . .
So open up your hardened hearts
    and let God enter in—

He only wants to help you
    a *new life to begin* . . .
And *every day's a good day*
    to lose yourself in others
And *any time a good time*
    to see mankind as brothers,
And this can only happen
    when you realize it's true
That *everyone needs someone*
    and that *someone is you!*

"Dear Friends"

"Dear Friends"

We all need words to live by,
To inspire us and guide us,
Words to give us courage
When the trials of life betide us—
And the words that never fail us
Are the words of God above,
Words of comfort and of courage
Filled with wisdom and with love—

They are ageless and enduring
They have lived through generations,
There's no question left unanswered
In Our Father's revelations—
And in this ever-changing world
God's words remain unchanged,
For though through countless ages
They've been often re-arranged,

The *truth* shines through all changes
Just as *bright today* as *when*
Our Father made the *Universe*
And breathed His Life in men—
And the words of inspiration
That I write for you today
Are just the old enduring truths
Said in a rhythmic way—

And if my "borrowed words of truth"
In some way touch your heart,
Then I am deeply thankful
To have had a little part
In sharing these *God-given lines,*
And I hope you'll share them, too,
With family, friends and loved ones
And all those dear to *you*.

If you enjoyed EVERYONE NEEDS SOMEONE, you'll want to read other collections of inspirational verse by Helen Steiner Rice—each one a beautifully-designed, clothbound gift-edition . . .

A GIFT OF LOVE

A treasury of beautiful poetry, handsomely-bound in white moire with illustrations throughout **$5.95**

HEART GIFTS from Helen Steiner Rice

A boxed, gift edition of poems with a frontis-piece and biographical sketch of the author. **$3.95**

LOVINGLY, Helen Steiner Rice

The author's enthusiasm and sincerity add a special something to the holidays of the year. **$3.95**

PRAYERFULLY

Moving prayer-poems of thanks, supplica-tion and devotion. **$3.95**

SOMEONE CARES:

Poems of Helen Steiner Rice

This best-selling volume is a collection of some of the most beautiful inspirational poetry of the twentieth century. **$6.95**
Keepsake Edition (gift-boxed) **$8.95**

THE STORY OF THE CHRISTMAS GUEST

A beautiful gift edition of the classic Christ-mas legend adapted to poetry for young and old. **$2.50**

ORDER FROM YOUR BOOKSTORE

If your bookstore does not stock these books, order from:

Fleming H. Revell Company Old Tappan, New Jersey 07675

(Add postage of 35¢ for first book, 10¢ for each additional book.)